American Shop Facade

アメリカン・ショップファサード

Restaurant & Bar page3~page78

Fashion & Beauty page79~page114

Specialty & Service page115~page153

Street furniture & Other page154~page160

Restaurant & Bar

レストラン Grimpa (Restaurant , Miami)

レストラン P.F. Chang's (Restaurant , Miami)

レストラン Rosa mexicano（Restaurant , Miami）

バー Let's make a daiquiri（Bar , Miami）

ジェラート店 Coco gelato（Gelato shop , Miami）

レストラン Pizza e cucina（Restaurant , Miami）

レストラン The Knife（Restaurant , Miami）

レストラン Rosa mexicano (Restaurant , Miami)

レストラン Dolores Lolita (Restaurant , Miami)

レストラン Hard rock cafe (Restaurant , Miami)　　　　ドリンクバー　ランチ Smoothie king / Baja fresh (Drink bar / Lunch , Miami)

レストラン The Oceanaire (Restaurant , Miami)

レストラン Iron sushi (Restaurant , Miami)

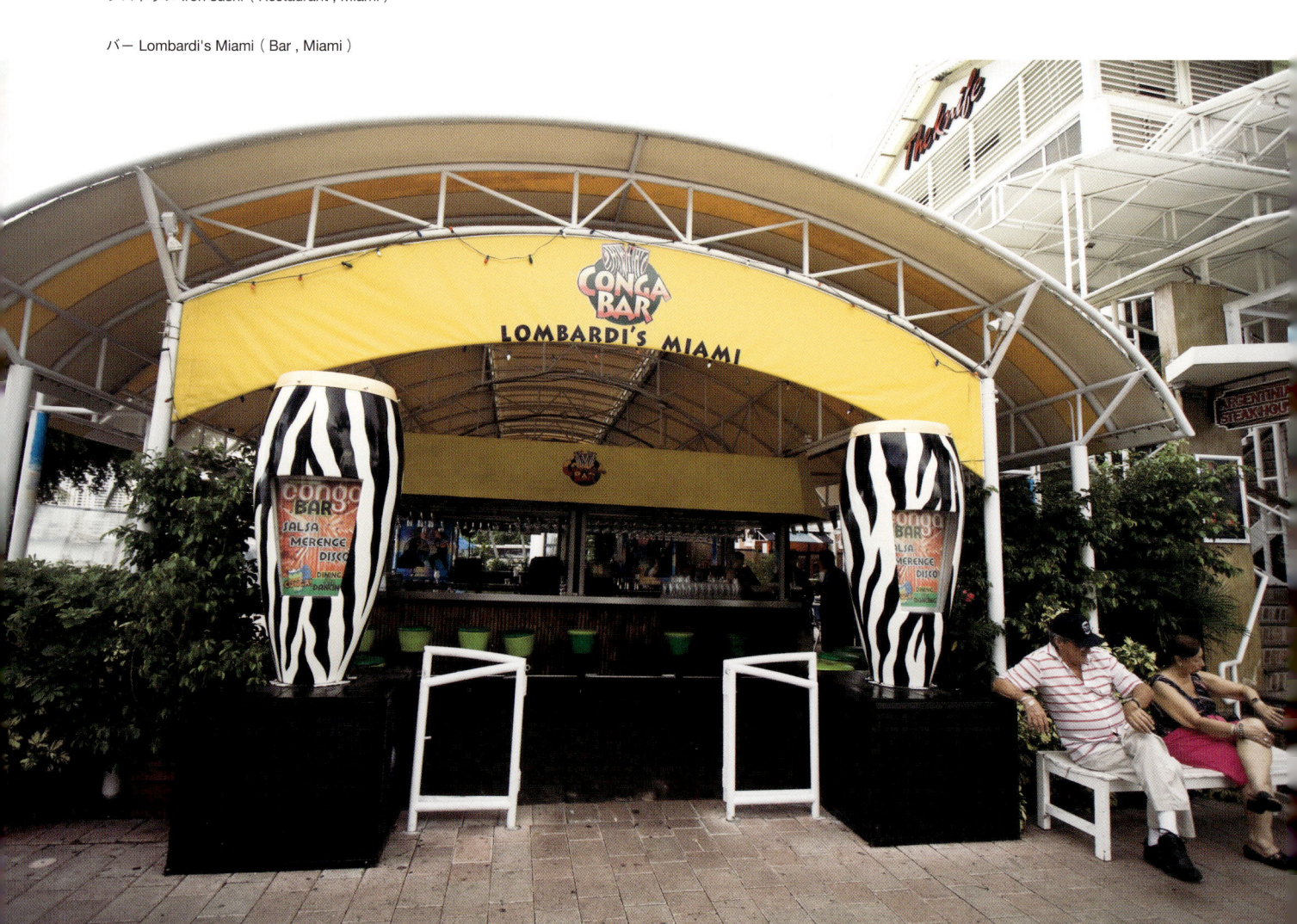

バー Lombardi's Miami (Bar , Miami)

バー Tequila chicas (Bar , Miami)

レストラン Subs grill (Restaurant , Miami)

レストラン Thai house (Restaurant , Miami)

レストラン Escopazzo (Restaurant , Miami)

レストラン Hosteria Romana (Restaurant , Miami)

レストラン Primarepa (Restaurant , Miami)

レストラン Sushi samba (Restaurant , Miami)

レストラン Ratatouille Bistro (Restaurant , Miami)

ダイナー Diner (Diner , Miami)

レストラン Pasha's (Restaurant , Miami)

カフェ World resource café (Café , Miami)

レストラン Score (Restaurant , Miami)

ジム　パブ Crunch / Playwright Irish pub (Gym / Pub , Miami)

カフェ Ghirardelli (Café , Miami)

レストラン Las vegas cuban cuisine (Restaurant , Miami)

レストランカフェ Balans (Restaurant café , Miami)

レストラン Unknown (Restaurant , Miami)

レストラン Bumble fish (Restaurant , Philadelphia)

レストラン Tangerine (Restaurant , Philadelphia)

レストラン One fourteen (Restaurant , Philadelphia)

レストラン Red sky (Restaurant , Philadelphia)

レストラン Uzu (Restaurant , Philadelphia)

ベーカリー店 Au bon pain (Bakery , Philadelphia)　　　レストラン Chloe (Restaurant , Philadelphia)

レストラン Heat (Restaurant , Philadelphia)

レストラン Mr. Bar stool (Restaurant , Philadelphia)

レストラン 222 (Restaurant , Philadelphia)

ベーカリー店 Star shine bakery（Bakery, Philadelphia）

レストラン Moshi moshi 18th（Restaurant, Philadelphia）

レストラン Chung king garden（Restaurant, Philadelphia）

レストラン Tokyo（Restaurant, Philadelphia）

バー Blarney（Bar, Philadelphia）

レストラン Lovash (Restaurant , Philadelphia)

バー O'neals (Bar , Philadelphia)

レストラン Patou (Restaurant , Philadelphia)

レストランバー Ly michael's (Restaurant bar , Philadelphia)

レストラン Anjou (Restaurant , Philadelphia)

レストラン Soho pizza (Restaurant , Philadelphia)

レストラン Ishkabibble's (Restaurant , Philadelphia)

レストランバー Paradigm (Restaurant bar , Philadelphia)

レストラン Privé (Restaurant , Philadelphia)

レストラン Philadelphia fish & company（Restaurant, Philadelphia）

ラウンジ Bijou（Lounge, Philadelphia）

レストラン Alma de cuba（Restaurant, Philadelphia）

レストラン Brasserie perrier（Restaurant, Philadelphia）

レストランバー Copabanana（Restaurant bar , Philadelphia）

レストランバー Jons（Restaurant bar , Philadelphia）

レストラン South street souvlaki（Restaurant , Philadelphia）

レストラン The Latest dish（Restaurant , Philadelphia）

レストラン Sonny's famous steaks（Restaurant , Philadelphia）

ラウンジ Caribbean lounge（Lounge , Philadelphia）

レストランバー Downey's（Restaurant bar , Philadelphia）

レストラン SOS（Restaurant, Philadelphia）

レストランバー Unknown（Restaurant bar, Philadelphia）

レストラン Goodburger（Restaurant, Philadelphia）

レストラン Amici（Restaurant, Philadelphia）

ダイナー Cosi（Diner, Philadelphia）

ラウンジ Vango（Lounge, Philadelphia）

フローズンヨーグルト店 Phileo yogurt (Frozen yogurt , Philadelphia)

レストランバー Alfa (Restaurant bar , Philadelphia)

バー North (Bar , Philadelphia)

パブ Mantra (Pub , Philadelphia)

レストラン Unknown (Restaurant , Philadelphia)

バー Bar noir (Bar , Philadelphia)

レストラン Il portico (Restaurant , Philadelphia)

バー Dom dom (Bar , Philadelphia)

レストラン Haru (Restaurant , Philadelphia)

レストラン Core de roma (Restaurant , Philadelphia)

カフェ Miami café (Café , Philadelphia)

レストラン Continental (Restaurant , Philadelphia)

レストラン Ruth's Chris steak house (Restaurant , Philadelphia)

カフェ Ing direct café (Café , Philadelphia)

ダイナー The Remedy (Diner , New York)

ダイナー The Remedy (Diner , New York)

ファストフード Song 7.2 (Fast-food , New York)

レストラン Unknown (Restaurant , New York)

バーレストラン Unknown (Bar restautant , New York)

レストラン Tony's (Restaurant , New York)

カフェ Seattle Café (Coffee shop , New York)

レストラン Public (Restaurant , New York)

アイスクリーム店 Rice to Riches (Ice cream shop , New York)

アイスクリーム店 Cold stone (Ice cream shop , New York)

ランチ店 Pax (Lunch , New York)

ラウンジ Sin Sin (Lounge , New York)

レストラン Natsumi (Restaurant , New York)

カフェ Thailand Cafe (Café , New York)

レストラン The Orchard (Restaurant , New York)

レストラン Nanking（Restaurant bar , New York）

バーレストラン Firefly（Bar restautant , New York）

レストランバー Belcourt（Restaurant bar , New York）

レストラン Toloache（Restaurant , New York）

フローズンヨーグルト店 Pinkberry（Frozen yogurt , New York）

レストランバー Hawaiian Tropic (Restaurant bar , New York)

バーレストラン Social（Bar restaurant , New York）

レストラン Big daddy's（Restaurant , New York）

レストラン Jackson hole（Restaurant , New York）

レストラン Eatery（Restaurant , New York）

レストラン El Centro（Restaurant , New York）

レストラン Mangia e Bevi（Restaurant , New York）

レストラン Thalia（Restaurant , New York）

レストラン Old San Juan（Restaurant , New York）

テイクアウト Luckys（Take-out , New York）

レストラン Chanpen（Restaurant , New York）

レストラン Noodles 28（Restaurant , New York）

レストラン Noodle Studio（Restaurant , New York）

レストラン Forum (Restaurant , New York)

レストラン Ciro (Restaurant , New York)

ステーキハウス Old Homestead (Steak house , New York)

バー Vintage (Bar , New York)

ダイナー The Diner (Diner , New York)

レストラン Unknown (Restaurant , New York)

アイスクリーム店 Tasti D lite（Ice creame shop , New York）

レストラン Uncle Nick's（Restaurant , New York）

レストラン Vespa（Restaurant , New York）

レストラン Mustang（Restaurant , New York）

レストラン Elio's（Restaurant , New York）

レストラン Valbella ristorante (Restaurant , New York)

レストラン Galil (Restaurant , New York)

レストラン Health alicious (Restaurant , New York)

テイクアウト Sakae sushi (Take-out , New York)

レストラン Momoya (Restaurant , New York)

レストラン Beyond (Restaurant , New York)

レストランカフェ Rancho café (Restaurant café , New York)

ベーカリー店 Hot & Crusty (Bakery shop , New York)

レストラン Ozu (Restaurant , New York)

レストランバー Tonic (Restaurant bar , New York)

バー Emerald Inn（Bar , New York）

レストラン Mr. Ginger（Restaurant , New York）

レストラン Ple（Restaurant , New York）

レストラン Bardouno（Restaurant , New York）

ベーグル店 Pick a bagel（Bagels , New York）

レストランバー Nanoosh（Restaurant bar , New York）

レストランパブ Doc. Watson's（Restaurant Pub , New York）

ファストフード Maoz（Fast-food , New York）

レストラン Monaco（Restaurant , New York）

レストラン Baraonda（Restaurant bar , New York）

レストラン Vynl（Restaurant , New York）

レストランバー The Neptune room（Restaurant bar , New York）

レストラン Roberto Passon（Restaurant , New York）

ダイナー Lenny's（Diner , New York）

ケーキ店 Crumbs（Cake shop , New York）

カフェ Beach cafe（Café , New York）

レストラン Land（Restaurant , New York）

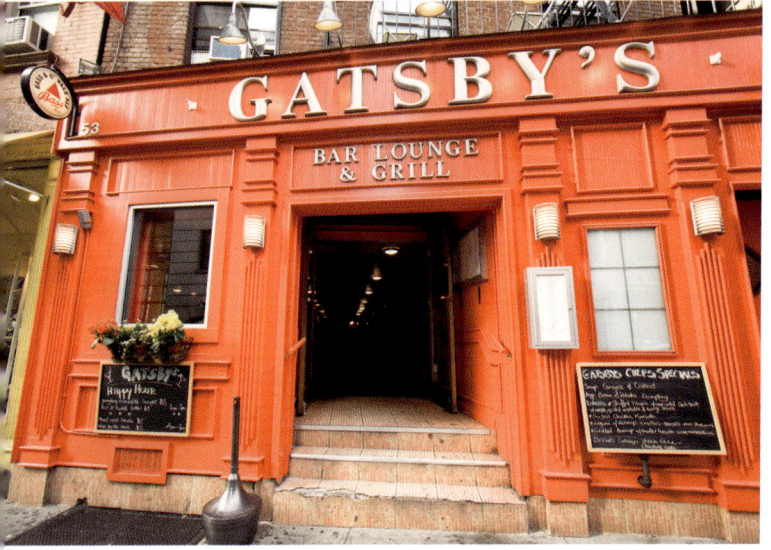

バー Gatsby's (Bar , New York)

レストラン Bread (Restaurant , New York)

カフェ Europan cafe (Café , New York)

レストラン Dishes (Restaurant , New York)

レストランカフェ Papillon (Restaurant café , New York)

ファストフード Quiznos Sub (Fast-food , New York)

レストラン Hummus place (Restaurant , New York)

レストラン Jacques (Restaurant , New York)

レストラン Rothmann's (Restaurant , New York)

レストラン La vela (Restaurant , New York)

レストランバー Junior's (Restaurant bar , New York)

バー Monkey bar (Bar , New York)

レストランバー Robert Emmetts (Restaurant bar , New York)

カフェ Prince St（Café , New York）

レストラン Unknown（Restaurant , New York）

レストラン Emilio's Ballato（Restaurant , New York）

ファストフード Subway（Fast-food , New York）

レストラン Al dente（Restaurant , New York）

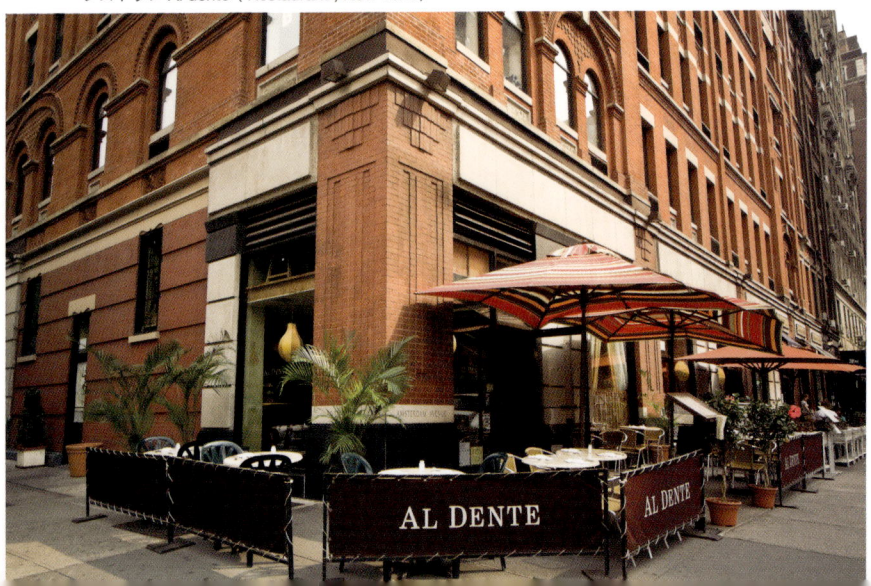

レストラン Barmarche（Restaurant , New York）

レストラン Financier（Restaurant , New York）

カフェ Café colonial（Café , New York）

バー Two eighteen（Bar , New York）

レストラン Parigot（Restaurant , New York）

ワインショップ 67 wine（Wine shop , New York）

レストラン Boi（Restaurant , New York）

バー Puck fair（Bar , New York）

カフェ Lucien（Café , New York）

レストラン Cafecito (Restaurant , New York)

レストラン Eleven B. (Restaurant , New York)

レストラン Unknown (Restaurant , New York)

カフェ Flea market café (Café , New York)

カフェ Cafe (Café , New York)

レストラン Accane (Restaurant , New York)

タバーン Whiskey Tavern (Tavern , New York)

カフェ Esperanto (Café , New York)

レストラン Akina sushi（Restaurant , New York）

レストラン Friend house（Restaurant , New York）

レストランバー Matilda（Restaurant bar , New York）

アイスクリーム店 Australian（Ice cream shop , New York）

レストラン Le Miu（Restaurant , New York）

バー E.U.（Bar , New York）

レストラン Lin's（Restaurant , New York）

ベーカリー店 Egg custard king café（Bakery , New York）

ベーカリー店 Grand 1 bakery（Bakery , New York）

レストラン Congee village（Restaurant , New York）

食品店 City gourmet（Food store , New York）

レストラン Mama（Restaurant , New York）

ファストフード Bite（Fast-food , New York）

レストラン East of 8th（Restaurant , New York）

レストラン Matsugen（Restaurant, New York）

レストラン Greenwich steak & bruger（Restaurant, New York）

レストラン Kori（Restaurant, New York）

レストラン Unknown（Restaurant, New York）

レストラン Sala（Restaurant, New York）

レストラン Unknown（Restaurant, New York）

カフェ Think coffee（Café, New York）

レストラン Rub BBQ (Restaurant , New York)

ダイナー Lenny's (Diner , New York)

ステーキハウス Uncle Jack's steakhouse (Restaurant , New York)

ファストフード Redhouse (Fast-food , New York)

レストラン Trailer park (Restaurant , New York)

レストラン Guacamole (Restaurant , New York)

ファストフード Homer's (Fast-food , New York)

レストラン Chipotle (Restaurant , New York)

レストラン Chipotle (Restaurant , New York)

ファストフード Dunkin' Donuts (Fast-food , New York)

バー Souths (Bar , New York)

レストラン Aceluck (Restaurant , New York)

フローズンヨーグルト店 Yo berry (Frozen yogurt , New York)

レストラン brgr (Restaurant , New York)

ファストフード Quiznos Sub (Fast-food , New York)

レストラン Thai select (Restaurant , New York)

レストラン Taste of Thai (Restaurant , New York)

ジュースバー Juice generation (Juice bar , New York)

レストラン Park (Restaurant , New York)

レストラン Arqua (Restaurant , New York)

ラウンジ Bungalo (Lounge , New York)

レストラン Thalassa (Restaurant , New York)

レストラン Unknown (Restaurant , New York)

レストラン Petrarca (Restaurant , New York)

レストラン Moran's (Restaurant , New York)

レストラン Morimoto（Restaurant , New York）

レストラン Flor de sol（Restaurant , New York）

レストラン Earth（Restaurant , New York）

レストラン U-choose express (Restaurant , New York)

カフェ Teariffic (Café , New York)

レストラン U-choose express (Restaurant , New York)

レストラン Yee Eng (Restaurant , New York)

ドリンクバー Vivi bubble tea (Drink bar , New York)

レストラン China Village (Restaurant , New York)

レストラン Hong Kong station (Restaurant , New York)

レストランバー Shanghai cuisine (Restaurant bar , New York)

レストラン Noodle village (Restaurant , New York)

ファストフード Atomic wings (Fast-food , New York)

ファストフード Quiznos Sub (Fast-food , New York)

レストラン Dallas BBQ (Restaurant , New York)

レストラン Bond 45 (Restaurant , New York)

ファミリーレストラン Applebee's (Restaurant bar , New York)

レストラン Spanky's BBQ (Restaurant , New York)

レストラン Ruby Tuesday (Restaurant , New York)

ファストフード Yoshinoya (Fast-food , New York)

レストラン Havana (Restaurant , New York)

レストラン Red lobster (Restaurant , New York)

ファストフード Girassoles（Fast-food , Miami）

バブ Paddy whacks（Pub , Philadelphia）

バー Sauza outlet（Bar , Miami）

ラウンジ Mojitos（Lounge , Miami）

カフェ Cafe nuvo（Café , Miami）

ファストフード Cosi（Fast-food , New York）

レストラン P.F. Chang's（Restaurant , Miami）

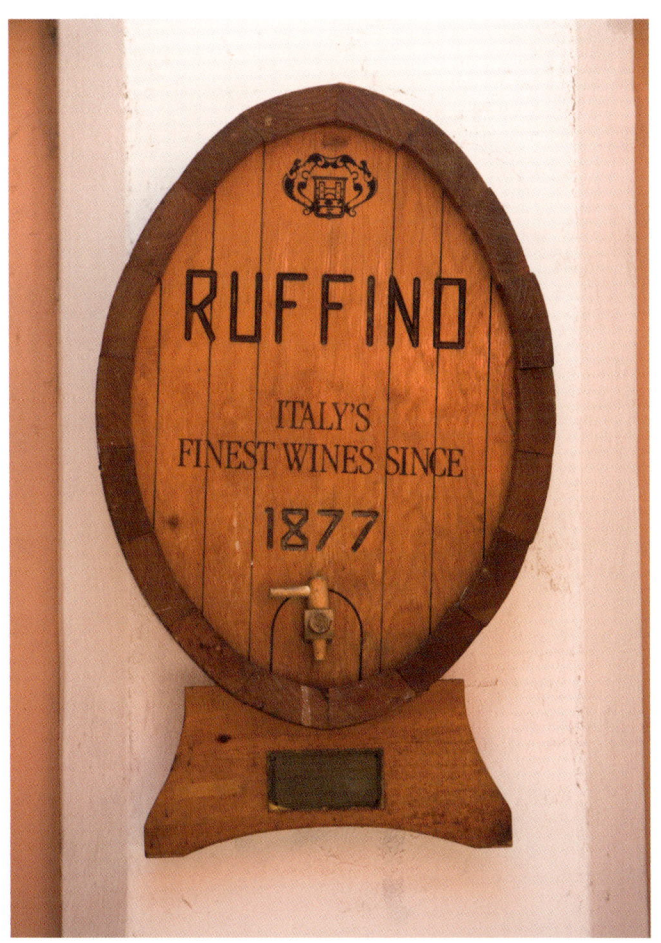

サイン Ruffino wine（Sign , Miami）

レストラン Oh Marco（Restaurant , Miami）

レストラン Adrienne's（Restaurant , New York）

レストラン Blú（Restaurant , Miami）

バー Monkey bar（Bar , New York）

コーヒーチェーン店 Seattle's best（Coffee chain , New York）

レストラン The Bean（Restaurant , New York）

レストランラウンジ Copa Miami（Restaurant lounge , Philadelphia）

カフェ Unknown（Café , New York）

レストラン Daltons（Restaurant bar , New York）

レストランバー Peasant（Restaurant bar , New York）

レストラン Bottom of the sea（Restaurant , Philadelphia）

ラウンジ Bijou (Lounge , Philadelphia)

ファストフード Dumpling Man (Fast-food , New York)

ダイナー The Diner (Diner , New York)

レストラン Dumpling bar (Restaurant , New York)

アイスクリーム店 Australian (Ice cream shop , New York)

レストラン Triada (Restaurant , Philadelphia)

ストアサイン Unknown (Store sign , Philadelphia)

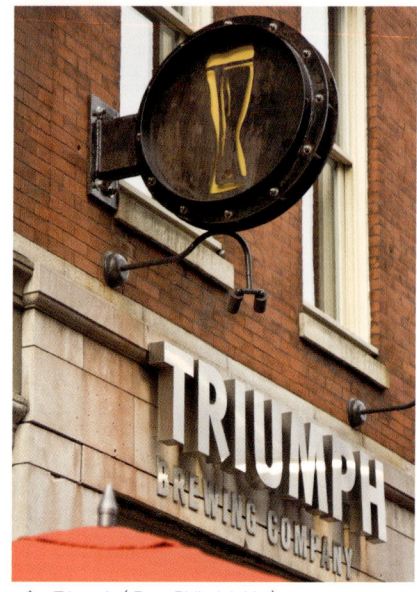

バー Triumph (Bar , Philadelphia)

レストランラウンジ Cebu
(Restaurant lounge , Philadelphia)

レストランバー Trade winds (Restaurant bar , Miami)

レストランバー Copabanana
(Restaurant bar , Philadelphia)

レストランバー Marmont (Restaurant bar , Philadelphia)

カラオケバー Planet Rose Karaoke (Karaoke Bar , New York)

レストラン Hosteria Romana (Restaurant , Miami)

ワインバー Ten degrees (Wine bar , New York)

レストラン The Other daiquiri bar (Restaurant , Miami)

レストラン Green grass (Restaurant , Miami)

レストラン Archie's (Restaurant , Miami)

レストラン Campo's (Restaurant , Philadelphia)

レストランバー Jons (Restaurant bar , Philadelphia)

カフェ Cafe nuvo（Café , Miami）

タパスバー Tapas & tintos（Tapas bar , Miami）

レストラン Siam cuisine（Restaurant , Philadelphia）

レストラン Lovely day（Restaurant , New York）

レストランバー Shanghai cuisine
（Restaurant bar , New York）

レストランラウンジ Gigi（Restaurant lounge , Philadelphia）

ラウンジ K（Lounge , New York）

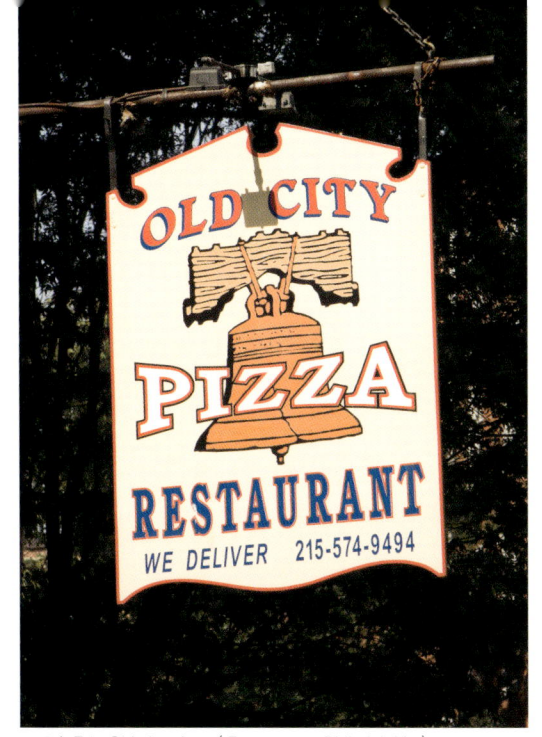

レストラン Old city pizza (Restaurant , Philadelphia)

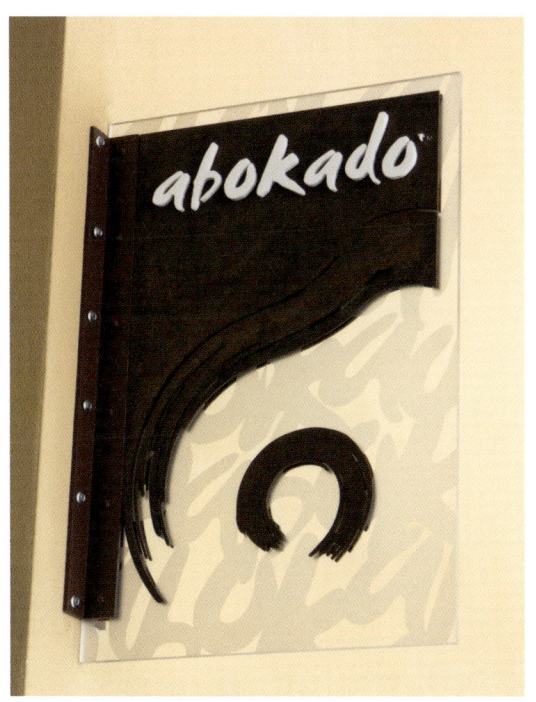

お茶店 Tea spot (Tea shop , New York)

レストラン Abokado (Restaurant , Miami)

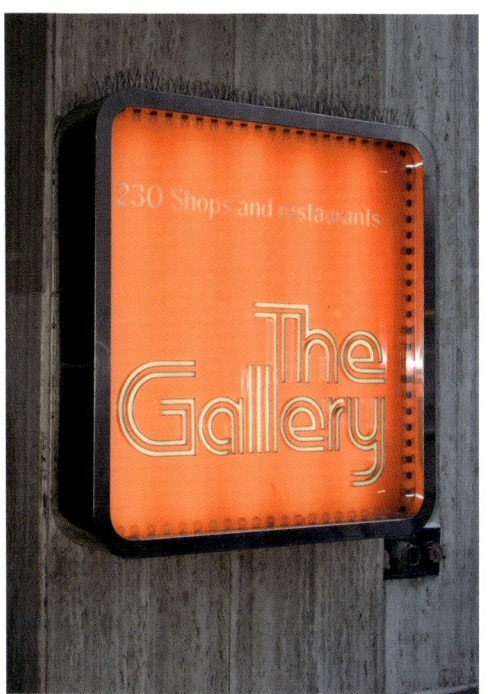

モールサイン The Gallery (Commercial complex , Philadelphia)

レストラン Table eight (Restaurant , Miami)

レストラン Unknown（Restaurant , Philadelphia） レストラン Unknown（Restaurant , Philadelphia）

レストラン Los ranchos（Restaurant , Miami）

レストラン Crown fried chicken（Restaurant , Philadelphia）

レストラン Hard rock cafe（Restaurant , Philadelphia） レストラン Trailer park（Restaurant , New York）

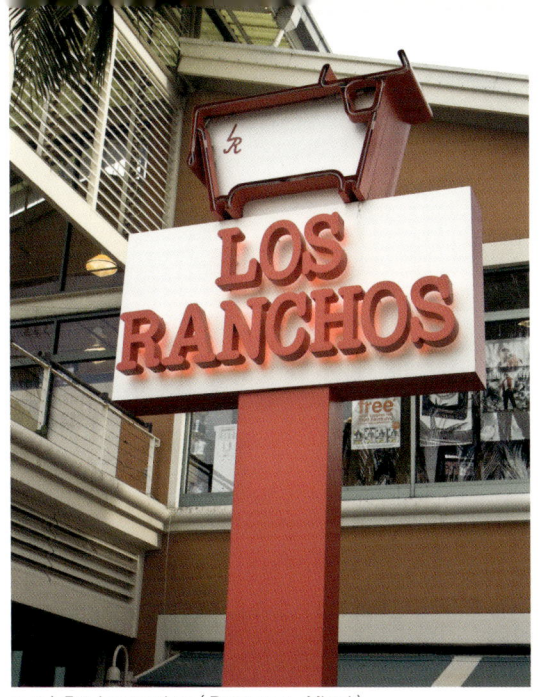

レストラン Los ranchos (Restaurant , Miami)

メニュー Bienvenidos (Menu , Miami)

ストアサイン Unknown (Store sign , Philadelphia)

カフェ Café Habana (Restaurant , New York)

バー Bar (Bar , Miami)

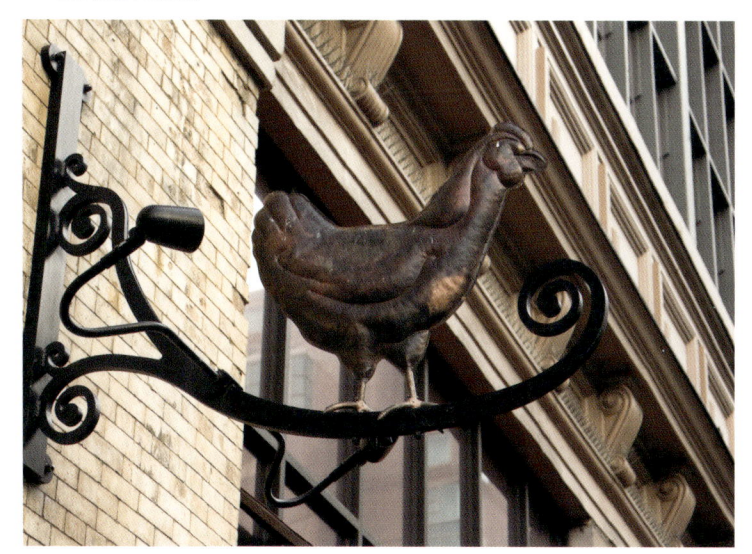

ストアサイン Unknown (Store sign , Philadelphia)

レストラン La Perrada (Restaurant , Miami)

ベーカリー店 Fresh on fifth（Bakery , Miami）

レストラン Fatburger（Restaurant , Miami）

レストラン Zen（Restaurant , Philadelphia）

レストラン Dunkin' Donuts（Restaurant , Philadelphia）

レストラン P.F. Chang's（Restaurant , Miami）

ジェラート店 Ro.ma（Gelato shop , Miami）

食品店 Despana（Food shop , New York）

Fashion & Beauty

貴金属 Claudian（Jewelry , Miami）

貴金属 Gold time（Jewelry , Miami）

靴店 Mixx（Shoe store , Miami）

ブティック BCBG Maxazria (Boutique , Miami)

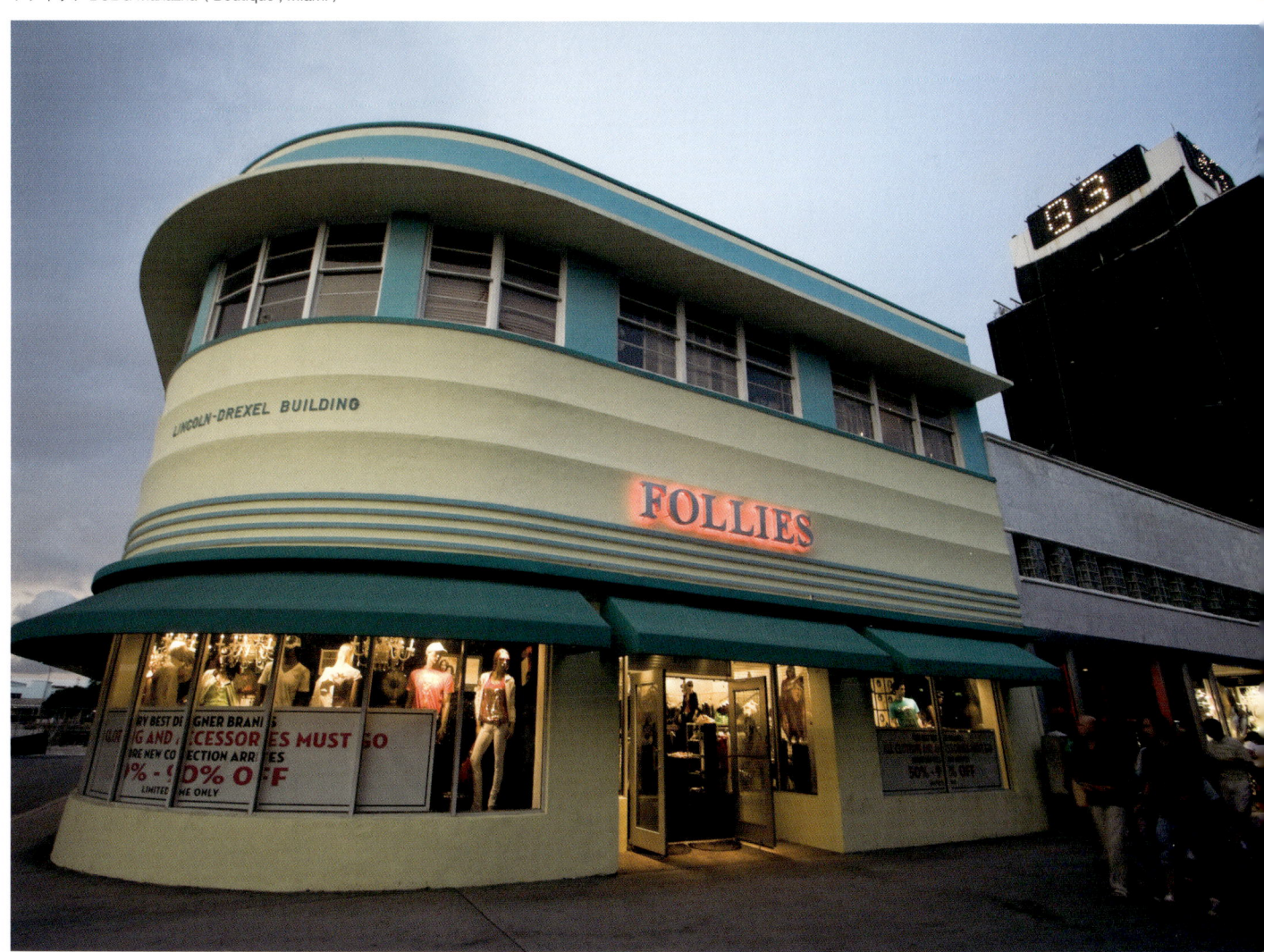

ブティック Follies (Boutique , Miami)

ブティック H&M (Boutique , Philadelphia)

ブティック Unknown (Boutique , Philadelphia)

ブティック Blanc de chine (Boutique , New York)

ブティック Ermenegildo Zegna (Boutique , New York)

ブティック Akris (Boutique , New York)

ブティック Fendi (Boutique , New York)

ブティック Tory Burch (Boutique , New York)

ブティック Astoria（Boutique , Miami）

ブティック Kenneth Cole（Boutique , Miami）

ヘアサロン L'atelier (Hair salon , Miami)

ヘアサロン Salon west (Hair salon , New York )　　　靴店 Marmi (Shoe store , New York)

ブティック Just cavalli (Boutique , New York)

ブティック Gant (Boutique , New York)

ブティック Adriano Goldschmied (Boutique , Miami)

ブティック Armani Exchange (Boutique , Miami)

ブティック Gap (Boutique , Miami)

ブティック Aldo (Boutique , Miami)

ボディショップ Sabon (Body shop , New York)

ブティック American apparel (Boutique , New York)

靴店 Moo Shoes (Shoe store , New York)

コスメティックス Lancome (Cosmetics , New York)

靴店 Unknown (Shoe store , New York)

ブティック Sample (Boutique , New York)

ヘアサロン用品 Yann Varin (Hair salon products , New York)

ブティック Calypso (Boutique , New York)

ブティック Loft（Boutique , New York）

古着店 Double rl（Vintage clothing store , New York）

ヘアサロン Crops for girls（Hair salon , New York）

帽子店 Lids（Cap shop , New York）

ブティック Theory (Boutique , New York)

コスメティックス MAC (Cosmetics , New York)

ブティック De grisogono（Boutique , New York）

靴店 Sigerson Morrison（Shoe store , New York）

靴店 Aerosoles (Shoe store , Philadelphia)

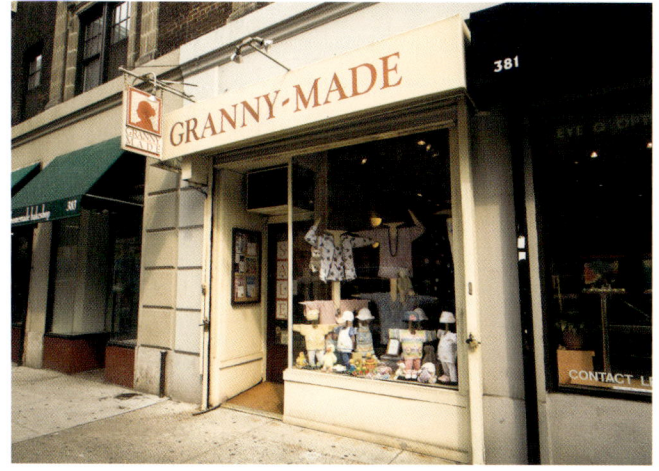

子供服 Granny-made (Children clothing , New York)

ブティック Lord Willy's (Boutique , New York)

靴店 John Fluevog (Shoe store , New York)

ブティック Poppy (Boutique , New York)

子供服 A time for children (Children clothing , New York)

靴店 Payless (Shoe store , Miami)

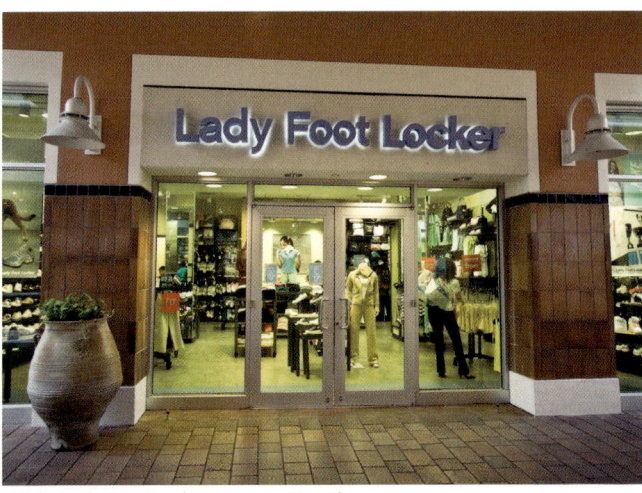

靴店 Lady Foot Locker (Shoe store , Miami)

ブティック Base (Boutique , Miami)

ブティック Miss sixty (Boutique , Miami)

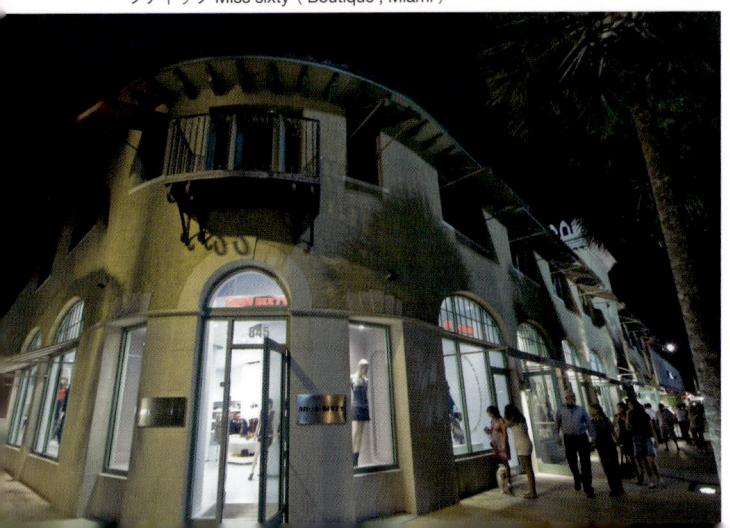

ブティック 579 (Boutique , Miami)

ブティック Rainbow (Boutique , Miami)

ブティック French connection (Boutique , Miami)

ブティック Loft (Boutique , Miami)

ブティック Napapijri (Boutique , Miami)

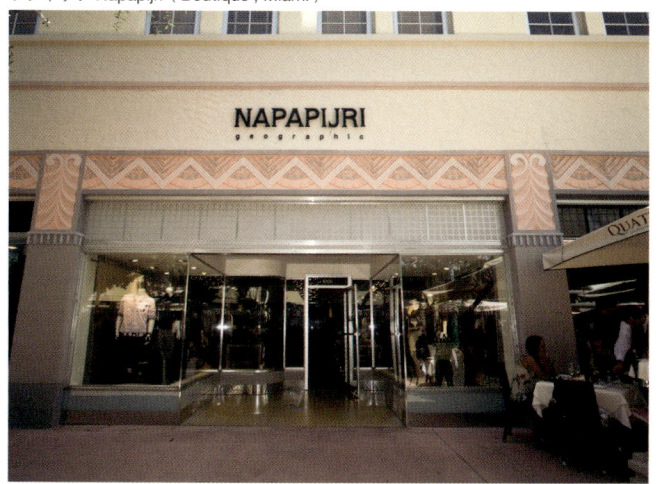

アクセサリー Barbara Palacios (Accessory shop , Miami)

ブティック Woldorf towers (Boutique , Miami)

ブティック Guess (Boutique , Miami)

ブティック Quick silver (Boutique , Miami)

ランジェリー Victoia's secret (Lingerie shop , Miami)

ブティック Deco collection (Boutique , Miami)

水着店 Zoon（Swim wear shop , Miami）

ブティック Diesel（Boutique , Miami）

ブティック The mood (Boutique , Philadelphia)

スポーツウエア Puma (Sports wear , Philadelphia)

靴店 Benjamin lovell Shoes (Shoe store , Philadelphia)

ブティック Diesel (Boutique , Philadelphia)

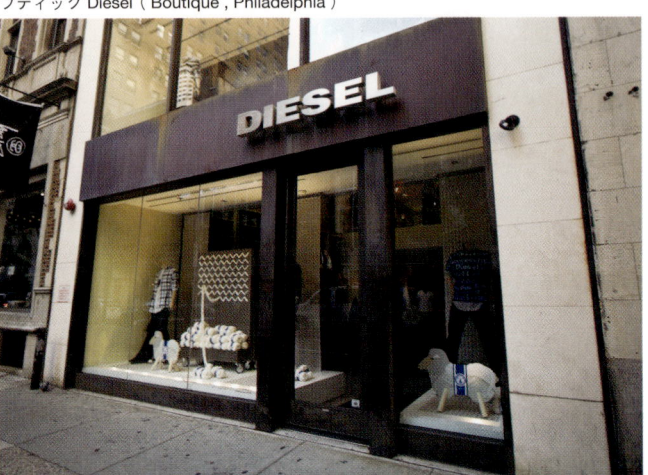

ブティック Net (Boutique , Philadelphia)

ヘアサロン East end (Hair salon , Philadelphia)

靴店 Payless (Shoe store , Philadelphia)

ジーンズショップ Charlie's (Jeans shop , Philadelphia)

ブティック Villa (Boutique , Philadelphia)

ヘアサロン Hair shapers（Hair salon , New York）

ヘアサロン Comfort zone（Hair salon , New York）

ブティック Mimi maternity（Boutique , Philadelphia）

ブティック Urban outfitters（Boutique , Philadelphia）

ブティック Arden b.（Boutique , Philadelphia）

ブティック Comme des garcons (Boutique , New York)

ブティック Unknown (Boutique , New York)

ブティック American apparel (Boutique , New York)

貴金属 B.tiff (Jewelry , New York)

ボディショップ Fresh (Body shop , New York)

美容室 Unknown (Beauty shop , New York)

アクセサリー Unknown (Accessory shop , New York)

靴店 Shoe (Shoe store , New York)

ブティック Namja Yeoja (Boutique , New York)

ランジェリー Coqueta (Lingeries shop , New York)

ブティック Balenciaga (Boutique , New York)

ブティック Unknown (Boutique , Philadelphia)

ブティック Agent (Boutique , Philadelphia)

ブティック Eye's gallery (Boutique , Philadelphia)

ブティック Temptation (Boutique , Philadelphia)

ブティック Smak parlour (Boutique , Philadelphia)

靴店 Journeys（Shoe store, New York）

ブティック Rebecca Taylor（Boutique, New York）

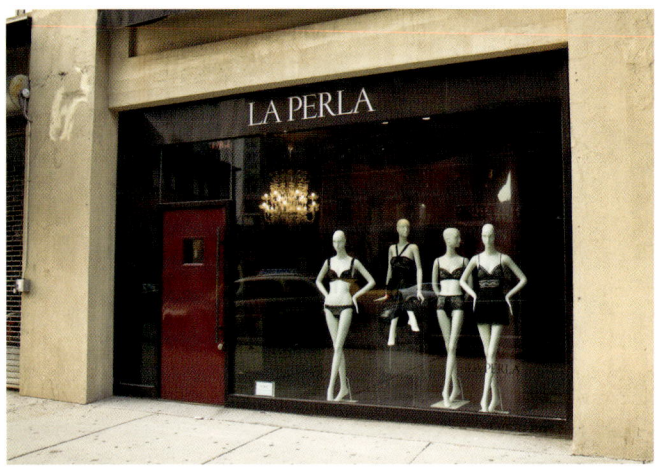

ランジェリー La Perla（Lingerie shop, New York）

ブティック Emmett McCarthy（Boutique, New York）

香水店 Le Labo（Fragrance shop, New York）

ブティック Earnest Sewn（Boutique, New York）

アクセサリー Gas bijoux（Accessory shop, New York）

ブティック Wear me out (Boutique , New York)

ブティック Miss sixty (Boutique , New York)

貴金属 Unknown (Jewelry , New York)

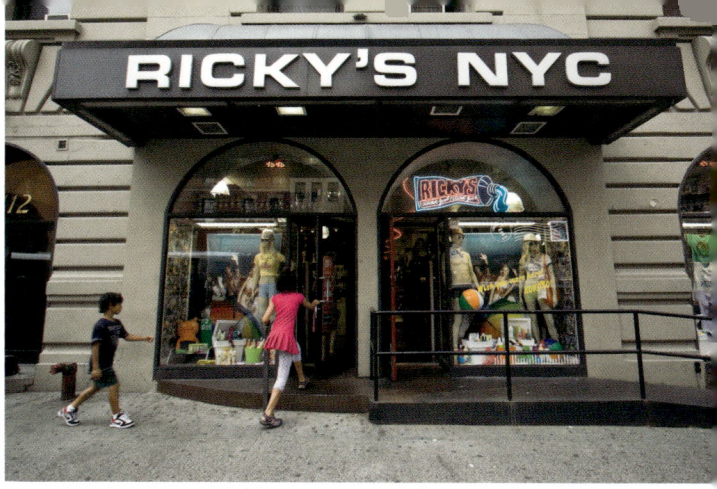

ジーンズショップ Earnest Sewn (Jeans shop , New York)

コスメティックス Ricky's NYC (Cosmetics , New York)

紳士服 Eleven (Menswear , New York)

靴店 Terra Plana (Shoe store , New York)

靴店 Crocs (Shoe store , New York)

アクセサリー Pinot (Accessory shop , Philadelphia)

ブティック South moon under (Boutique , Philadelphia)

靴店 Benjamin lovell Shoes (Shoe store , Philadelphia)

靴店 Station (Shoe store , Philadelphia)

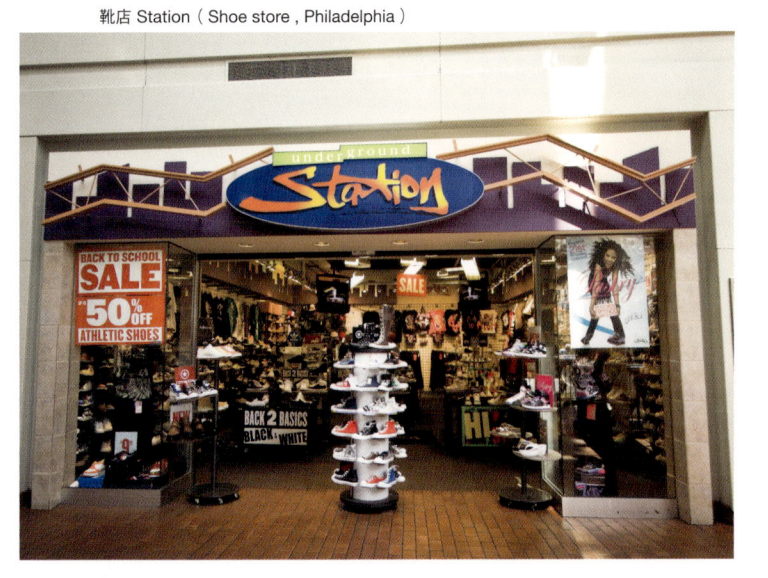

貴金属 Made by hand (Jewelry , Philadelphia)

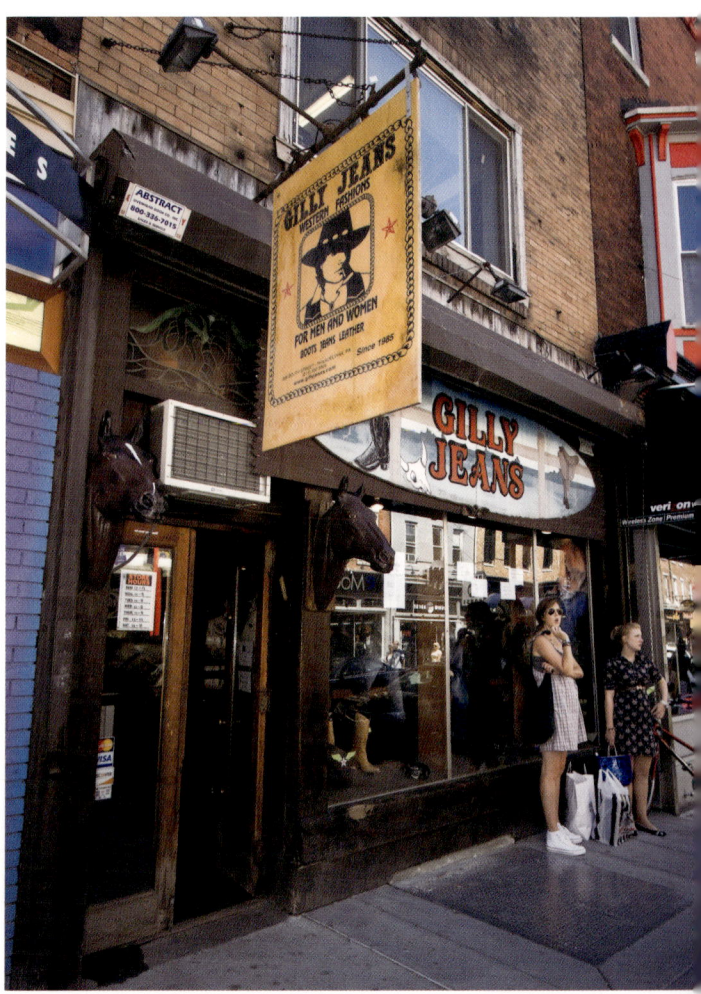

ジーンズショップ Gilly jeans (Jeans shop , Philadelphia)

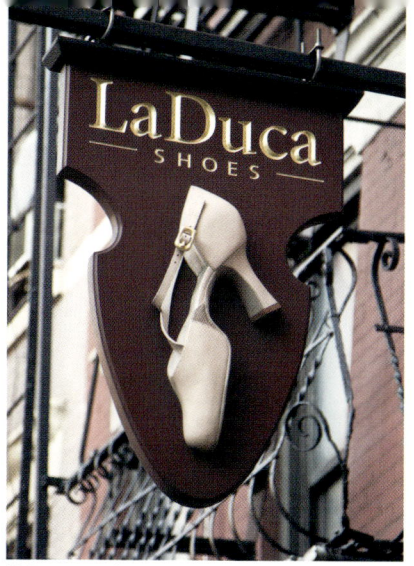

靴店 La Duca (Shoe store , New York)

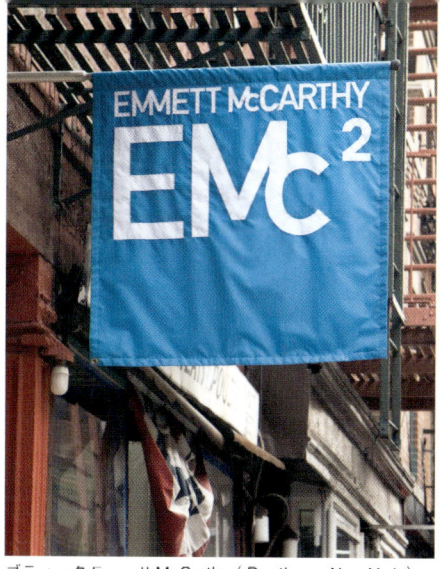

ブティック Emmett McCarthy (Boutique , New York)

水着店 Bayside Sun (Swim wear shop , Miami)

子供服 Kidville (Children clothing , New York)

ブティック Physical graffiti (Boutique , New York)

アクセサリー Le Bowtique (Accessory shop , Miami)

ブティック Ross (Boutique , Philadelphia)

貴金属 So good（Jewelry , Miami）

ブティック Tonke（Boutique , New York）

ブティック Seize sur Vingt Groupe（Boutique , New York）

ブティック Threads（Boutique , New York）

貴金属 Sowinski（Jewelry , Miami）

靴店 Xot（Shoe store , Miami）

アクセサリー Teno（Accessory shop , Miami）

Specialty & Service

コンドミニアム Unknown (Condominium , Miami)

コンドミニアム 1500 Ocean drive (Condominium , Miami)

眼鏡店　ジュースバー Sunglass hut / Ocean juice（Fashion optical / Juice bar , Miami）

ブティックホテル Unknown（Boutique hotel , Miami）

複合ビル Unknown (Commercial complex , Miami)

複合ビル Vidal sassoon / Sisley / Benetton (Complex building , Miami)

コミュニティプレイス Americas trade center (Community place , Miami)

エンターテインメント World erotic art museum (Entertainment , Miami)

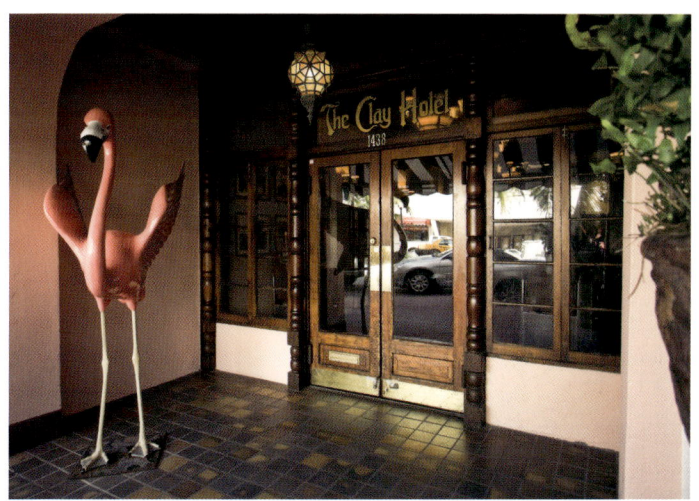

ブティックホテル The clay hotel (Boutique hotel , Miami)

ヨガスタジオ Pure (Yoga studio , New York)

スパ Metro spa (Spa , New York)

スパ Christine Chin Spa (Spa , New York)

スパ Spa Ology (Spa , New York)

時計店 Fossil（Watch shop , New York）

ダンススタジオ Duke（Dance studios , New York）

家具 Craig Van Den Brulle（Furniture store , New York）

眼鏡店 Lens crafters（Optical shop , New York）

州立複合ビル Pennsylvania convention center（State complex building , Philadelphia）

州立複合ビル Independence visitor center（State complex building , Philadelphia）

サロンスパ Tabu（Salon spa , Philadelphia）

ショールーム China glass silver（Showroom , Philadelphia）

ギャラリー Clay studio（Gallery , Philadelphia）

家具 Calligaris（Furniture store , Philadelphia）

旅行代理店 Gil travel（Travel agency , Philadelphia）

家具 Area id（Furniture , New York）

複合ビル National（Commercial complex , Philadelphia）

旅行代理店 Liberty travel（Travel agency , Philadelphia）

コマーシャルスペース Unknown (Commercial space , Miami)

ブティックホテル Victor（Boutique hotel , Miami）

ブティックホテル Claremont（Boutique hotel , Miami）

複合ビル Yuca（Commercial complex , Miami）

ブティックホテル Essex house（Boutique hotel , Miami）

複合ビル Sony music（Commercial complex , Miami）

コンピュータショップ Apple store Miami (Computer store , Miami)

ギャラリー Center south florida (Gallery , Miami)

写真ギャラリー Peter Lik (Gallery , Miami)

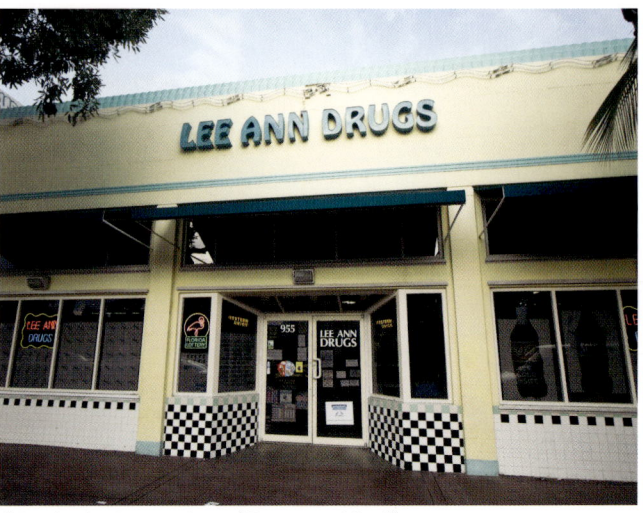

グッズ 9th Chakra (Goods , Miami)

ドラックストア Lee ann drugs (Drug store , Miami)

ブティックホテル Ocean five hotel（Boutique hotel , Miami）

ブティックホテル Lily（Boutique hotel , Miami）

ブティックホテル Cardozo hotel（Boutique hotel , Miami）

タトゥーラウンジ Tattoo lounge（Tattoo lounge , Miami）

複合ビル Unknown（Commercial complex , Miami）

映画館 Clearview（Movie theater, New York）

香り店 Red flower (Scents store , New York)

ネイルサロン Dashing diva (Nail salon , New York)

ギャラリー Unknown (Gallery , New York)

ギャラリー Unknown (Gallery , New York)

コメディーシアター Comix (Comedy theater , New York)

ギャラリー Art in general (Gallery , New York)

ショールーム Silas seandel (Show room , New York)

花屋 Unknown (Flower shop , New York)

ブティックホテル Blue Moon (Boutique hotel , New York)

携帯電話 at&t (Cellular phone , Philadelphia)

スパ Spa belles (Spa , New York)

コスチューム店 Mineralistic (Costume store , Philadelphia)

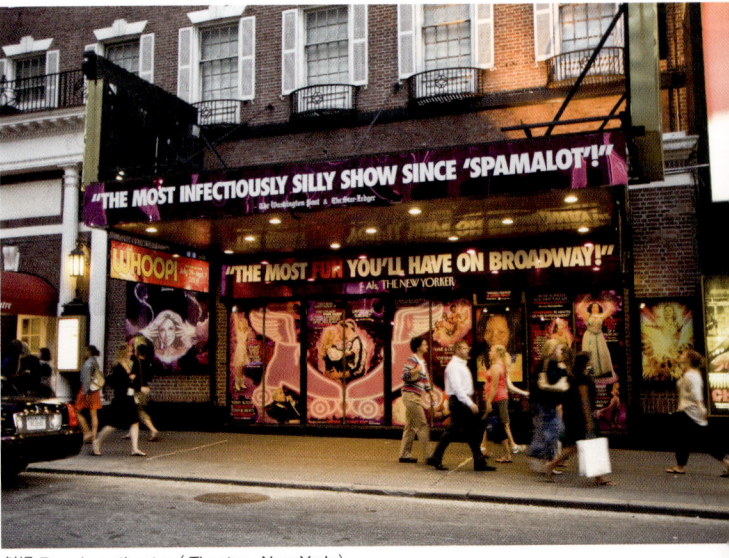

劇場 Broadway theater (Theater , New York)

照明器具 Unknown (Lighting store , Philadelphia)

グッズ Jinxed (Goods , Philadelphia)

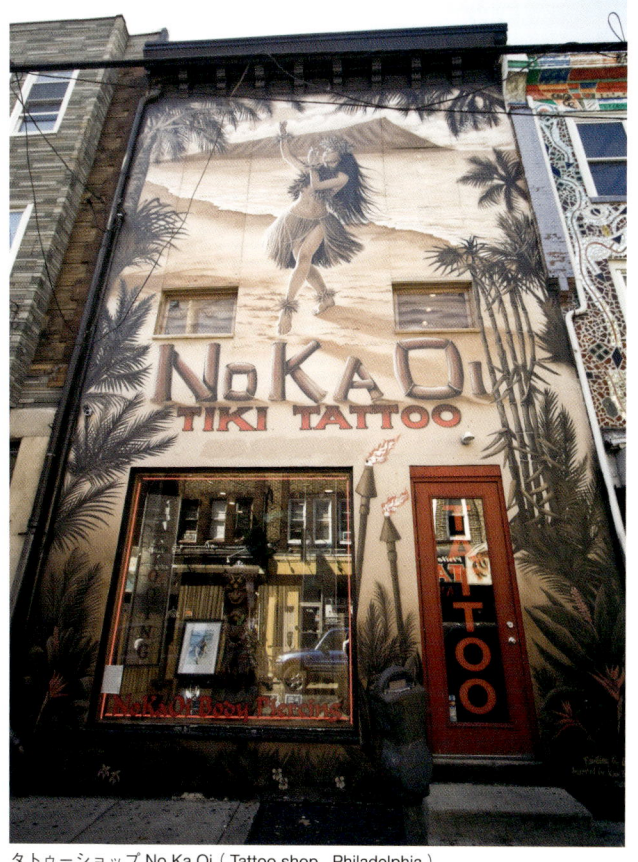

タトゥーショップ No Ka Oi (Tattoo shop , Philadelphia)

土産物店 New York（Gift store , New York）

コピーショップ Ibu copy（Copy shop , New York）

キャラクターグッズ Sanrio（Charactor goods store , New York）

ネイル＆スパ Spazio（Nail & spa , New York）

ポップコーン Garrett（Popcorn shop , New York）

食品店 Burgers & cupcakes (Food shop , New York)

パーティーグッズ Make (Party goods shop , New York)

雑貨店 Pylones (Goods , New York)

エンターテインメント Psychic / Flame job (Entertainment , New York)

ギャラリー Unknown (Gallery , New York)

電気・カメラ店 Audio cameras electronics（Electronics store , Miami）

劇場 Colony theater（Theater , Miami）

シガーショップ Deco drive cigars（Cigar shop , Miami）

スケート店 M.I.A（Sketeshop , Miami）

劇場 Pottery barn（Theater, Miami）

タトゥーショップ Tattoo（Tattoo shop, Miami）

ファーマシー CVS pharmacy（Pharmacy, Miami）

リカーストア 69st Liquors（Liquor store, Miami）

ブティックホテル Shelley（Boutique hotel, Miami）

ブティックホテル Chesterfield（Boutique hotel, Miami）

ブックストア Borders（Book store , New York）

携帯電話 Helio（Cellular phone , New York）

ギャラリー Unknown（Gallery , New York）

眼鏡店 Mao chang（Optics , New York）

装飾店 Stella（Home décor , New York）

家具 Mitchell Gold + Bob Williams（Furniture , New York）

眼鏡屋 Linda Derector（Optical shop , New York）

花店 Manhattan florist, inc.（Flower shop , New York）

審美歯科 Vital dent（Cosmetic dentistry , New York）

ワインストア Appellation（Wine store , New York）

ファーマシー Kiehl's（Pharmacy , New York）

コメディー劇場 Gotham（Comedy theater , New York）

審美歯科 Vital dent（Cosmetics dentistry , New York）

印刷店 Digital Printing（Printing , New York）

カメラ店 Ritz camera（Camera shop , New York）

銀行支店 Capital One Bank（Bank branch , New York）

銀行支店 Capital One Bank（Bank branch , New York）

携帯電話 Tmobile（Cellular phone , New York）

銀行支店 Chase（Bank branch , New York）

銀行支店 First Republic Bank（Bank branch , New York）

ゲーム店 Game stop（Game shop , New York）

写真店 86 street photo（Photoshop , New York）

ドラッグストア Duane reade（Drug store , New York）

食品店 Trader joe's（Food store , New York）

カーディーラー Hummer (Car dealer , New York)

カーディーラー Major (Car dealer , New York)

カーディーラー Major (Car dealer , New York)

ニューススタンド Newsstand (Newsstand , New York)

ニューススタンド Newsstand (Vender , Philadelphia)

ブティックホテル White law (Boutique hotel , Miami)

ブティックホテル Park central hotel (Boutique hotel , Miami)

ブティックホテル Beach paradise (Boutique hotel , Miami)

ブティックホテル The Tides (Boutique hotel , Miami)

ギャラリー 3 floors of art (Gallery , Miami)

銀行支店 Citibank (Bank branch , Miami)

劇場 Lincolin theatre (Theater , Miami)

ブティックホテル Cavalier (Boutique hotel , Miami)

ブティックホテル Barolo (Boutique hotel , Miami)

ブティックホテル Unknown (Boutique hotel , Miami)

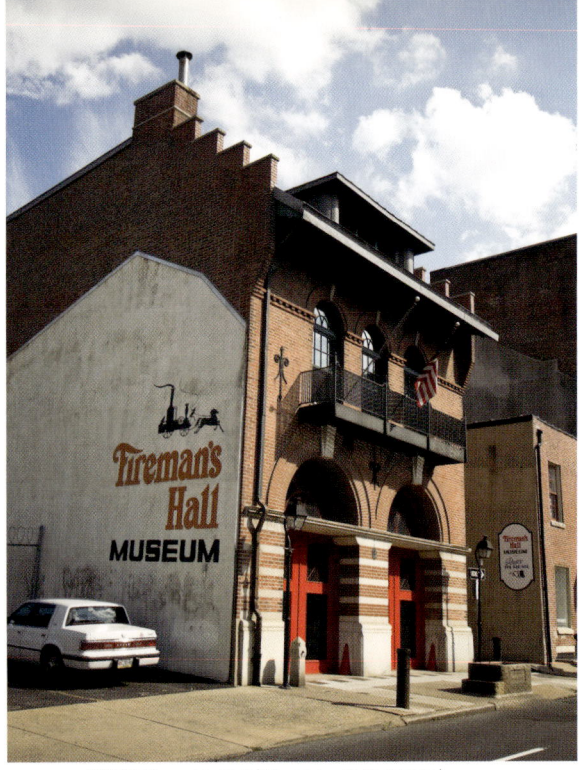

博物館 Fireman's hall (Museum , Philadelphia)

旗店 Humphrys flag co. (America's oldest flag store since 1874 , Philadelphia)

ショールーム Economy (Showroom , Philadelphia)

ペットショップ Doggie style (Pet shop , Philadelphia)

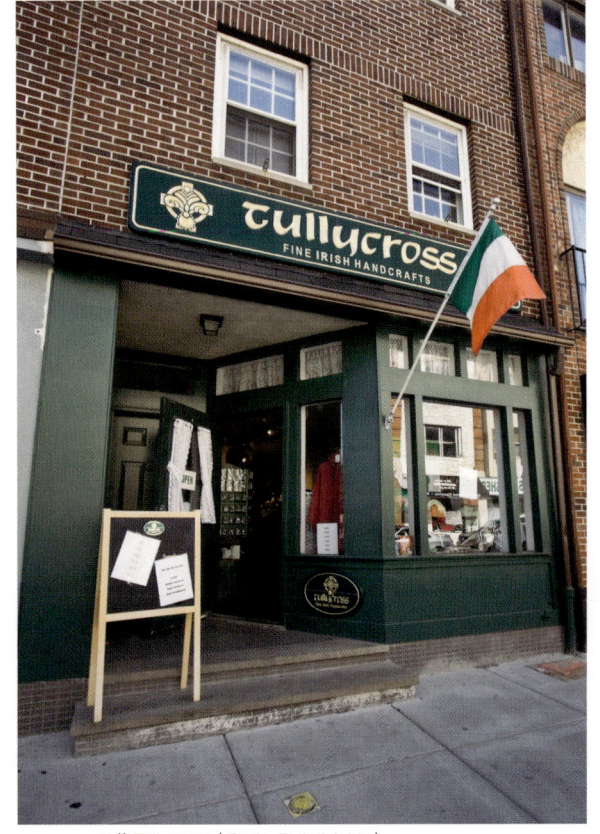

工芸 Tullycross (Craft , Philadelphia)

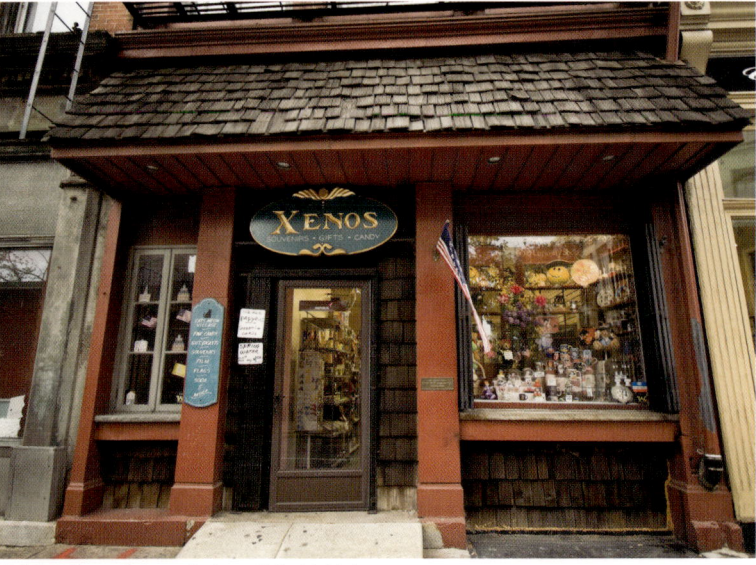

土産物店 Xenos (Souvenir shop , Philadelphia)

コンビニエンスストア Wawa（Convenience store, Philadelphia）

劇場 Philadelphia theatre company（Theater, Philadelphia）

携帯電話 Tmobile（Cellular phone, Philadelphia）

眼鏡店 eyechic（Fashion optical, Philadelphia）

携帯電話 Sprint（Cellular phone, Philadelphia）

銀行支店 Conestoga bank（Bank branch, Philadelphia）

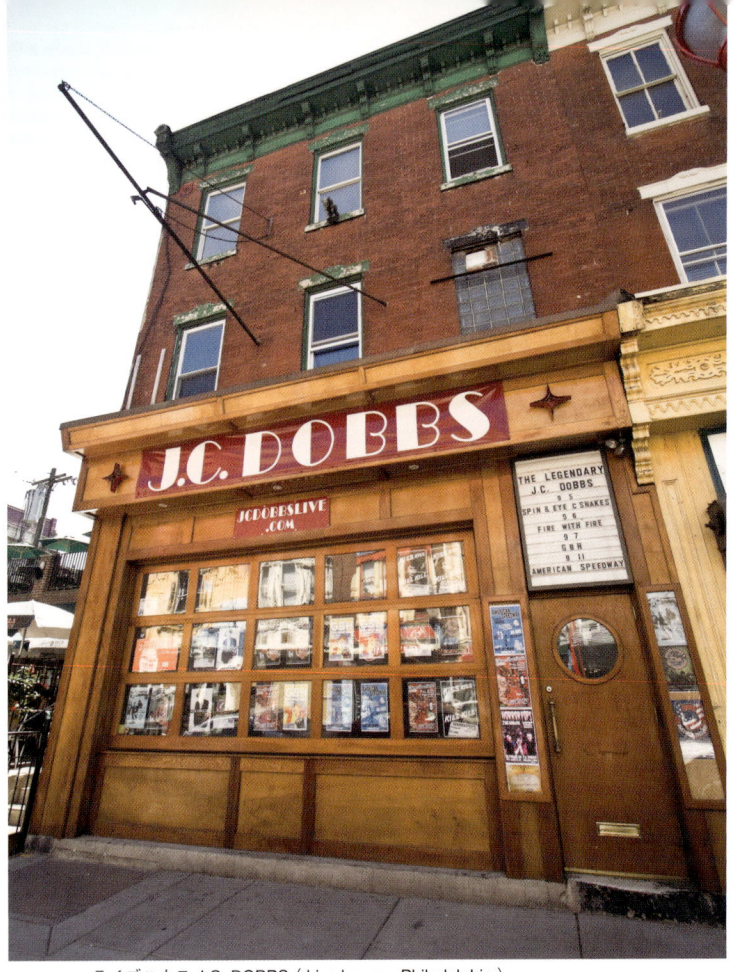

ライブハウス J.C. DOBBS (Live house , Philadelphia)

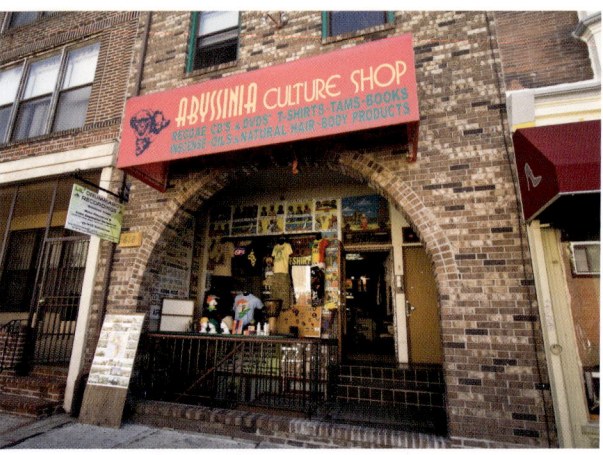

グッズ Abyssinia culture shop (Goods , Philadelphia)

携帯電話 Mobile zone (Cellular phone , Philadelphia)

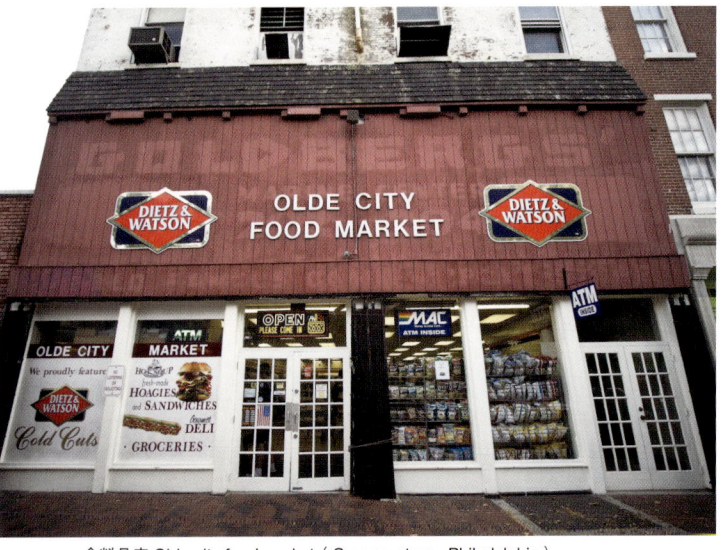

食料品店 Olde city food market (Grocery store , Philadelphia)

スパ Tai chi (Spa , Philadelphia)

レコードショップ Funk o mart (Record shop , Philadelphia)

自転車店 Bike line (Bicycle shop , Philadelphia)

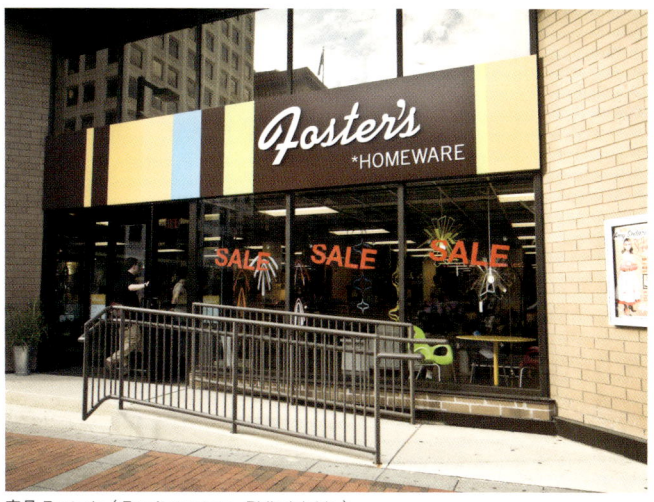

家具 Foster's（Furniture store , Philadelphia）

アートサプライ Art supplies（Art supplies , Philadelphia）

デザイン事務所 Sign a rama（Design office , Philadelphia）

ペットショップ Accent on animals（Pet shop , Philadelphia）

スポーツグッズ Olympia sports（Sports goods , Philadelphia）

タトゥーショップ Tattooing（Tattoo shop , Philadelphia）

調理器 Swift（Food equipment store , Philadelphia）

陶器店 Steap（Ceramic store , Philadelphia）

複合ビル Reading terminal market（Commercial complex , Philadelphia）

映画館 Regal cinemas（Movie theater , New York）

アミューズメント館 Ripley's Believe it or not（Amusement place , New York）

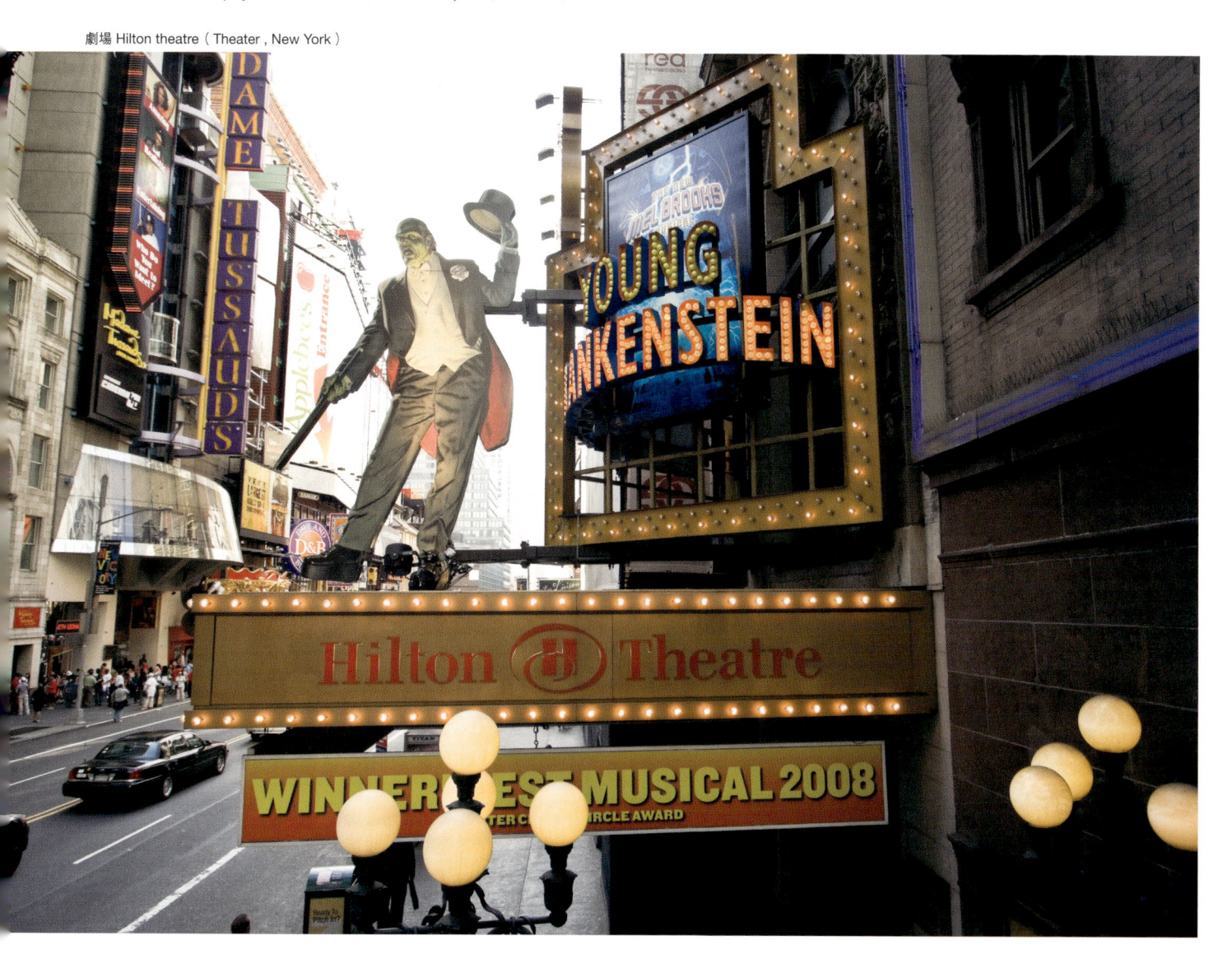

劇場 Hilton theatre（Theater , New York）

土産物店 Wings（Souvenir shop, Miami）

ブティックホテル Clinton（Boutique hotel, Miami）

劇場 Mamma mia（Theater, New York）

銀行ビルボード Wachovia（Bank billbord, New York）

銀行支店 Great Florida Bank（Bank branch, Miami）

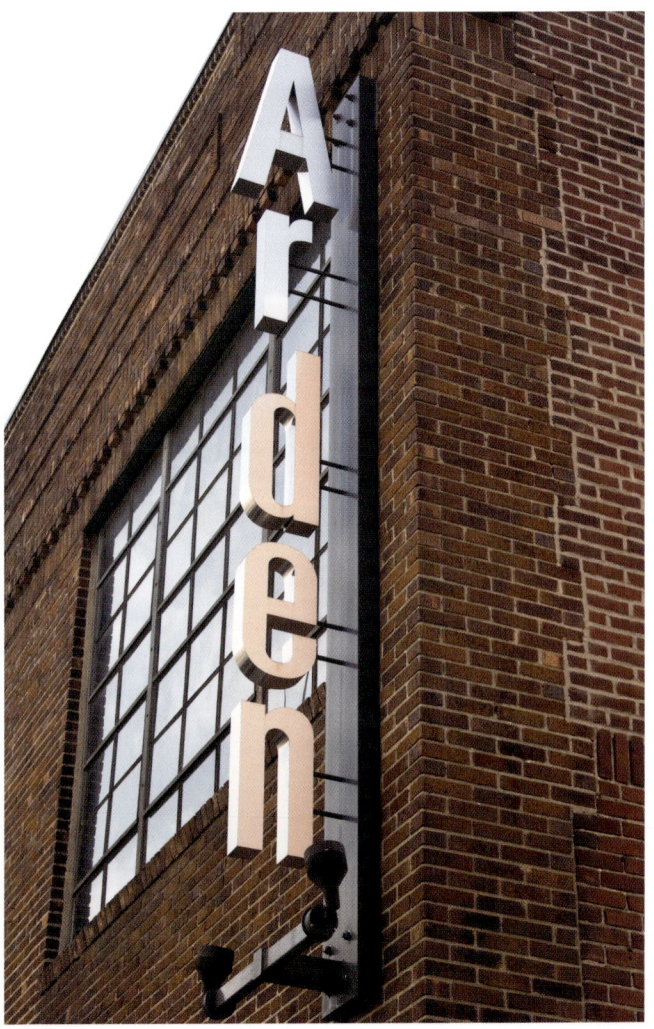

劇場 Arden（Theater, Philadelphia）

複合ビル Unknown (Commercial complex , Miami)

ブティックホテル De Soleil (Boutique hotel , Miami)

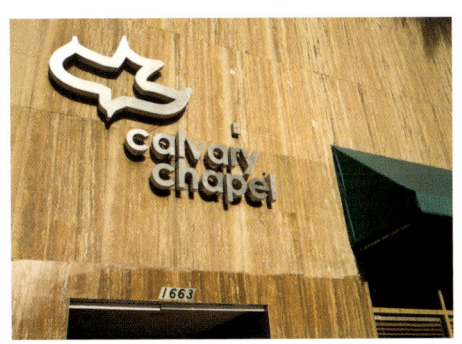

チャペル Calvary chapel (Chapel , Miami)

ブティックホテル De Soleil (Boutique hotel , Miami)

博物館 Fireman's hall (Museum , Philadelphia)

ブティックホテル Albion (Boutique hotel , Miami)

ブティックホテル The Catalina (Boutique hotel , Miami)

コンドミニアム Camden (Condominium , Miami)

土産物店 Passage to India（Souvenir shop , New York）

土産物店 The Tin man,（Souvenir shop , Miami）

家具 Okooko（Furniture store , Philadelphia）

土産物店 Miami's for me（Souvenir shop , Miami）

旗店 World of Flags（Flag shop , Miami）

土産物店 Orient station（Souvenir shop , Miami）

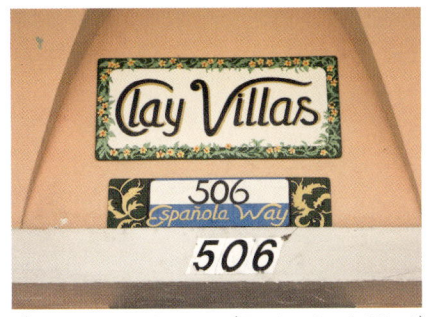

ブティックホテル Clay Villas（Boutique hotel, Miami）

カード ギフト Delphinium（Cards and gifts, New York）

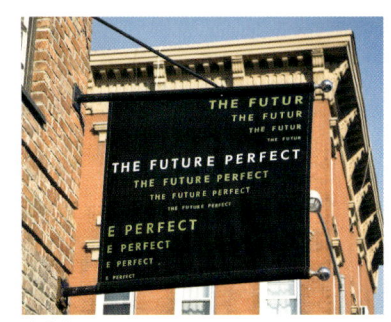

家具店 The future perfect（Furniture store, New York）

家具 Craig Van Den Brulle（Furniture, New York）

ヨガスタジオ Synergy（Yoga studio, Miami）

食品店 Cellini（Food shop, New York）

アートクラフト American pie（Arts&crafts, Philadelphia）

土産物店 Best of Miami（Souvenir shop, Miami）

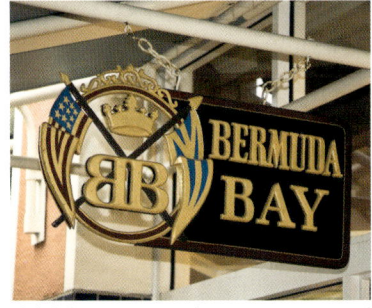

土産物店 Bermuda bay（Souvenir shop, Miami）

土産物店 Art by god（Souvenir shop, Miami）

時計店 World time（Watch shop, Miami）

ペットショップ Puppies（Pet shop, Miami）

眼鏡店 Izone（Fashion optical, Miami）

土産物店 Bayside cigars（Souvenir shop, Miami）

ビーチグッズ All you need to reach the beach（Beach goods, Miami）

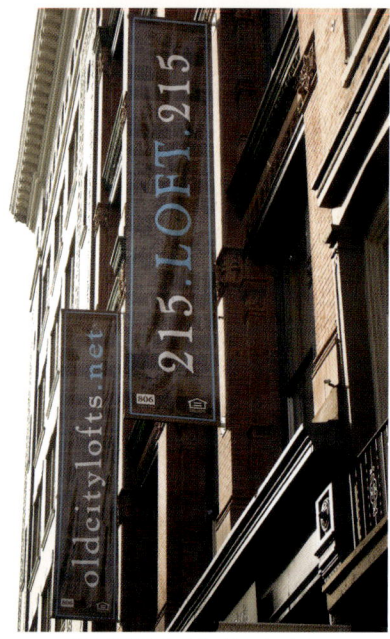

不動産 Old city lofts（Real estate, Philadelphia）

ブティックホテル Stardust apts（Boutique hotel, Miami）

ホテル Independence park（Hotel, Philadelphia）

ブックストア Read（Book store, New York）

ブックストア 192Books（Book store, New York）

コメディークラブ HA!（Comedy club, New York）

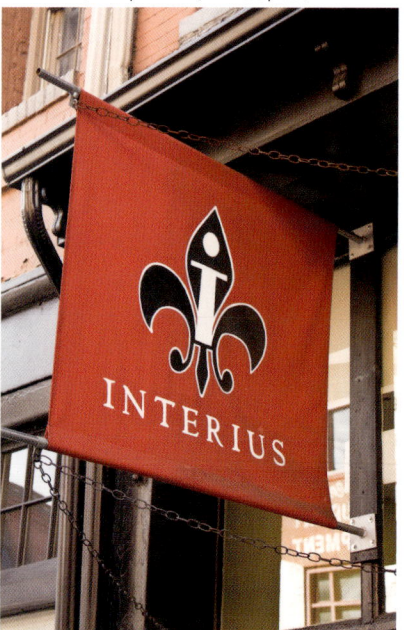

アンティーク Interius（Antique store, Philadelphia）

保険サイン Butrus & whalon（Insurance, Philadelphia）

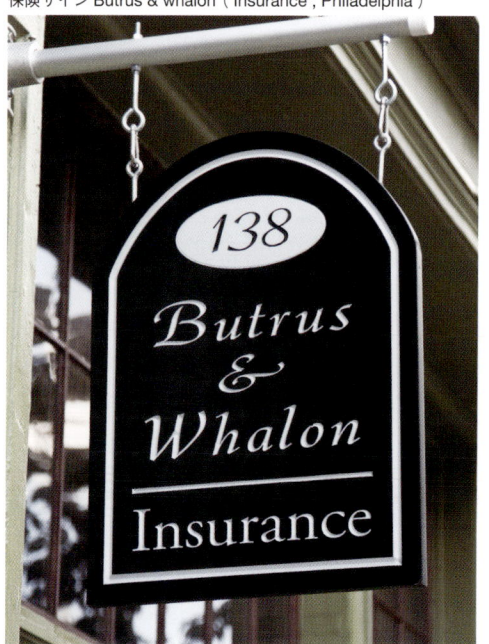

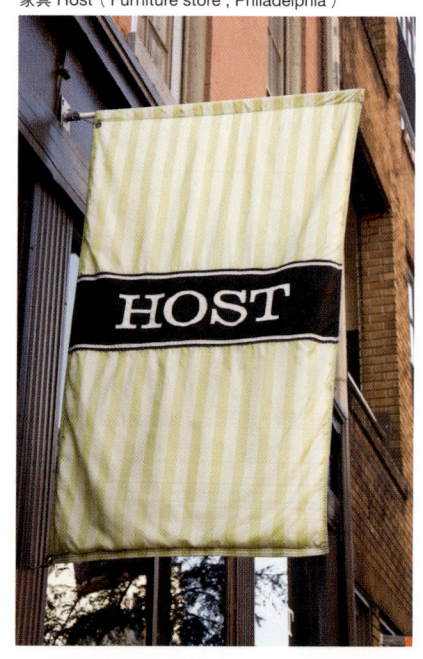

家具 Host（Furniture store, Philadelphia）

ホールセール Second St. whole sale (Whole sale , Philadelphia)

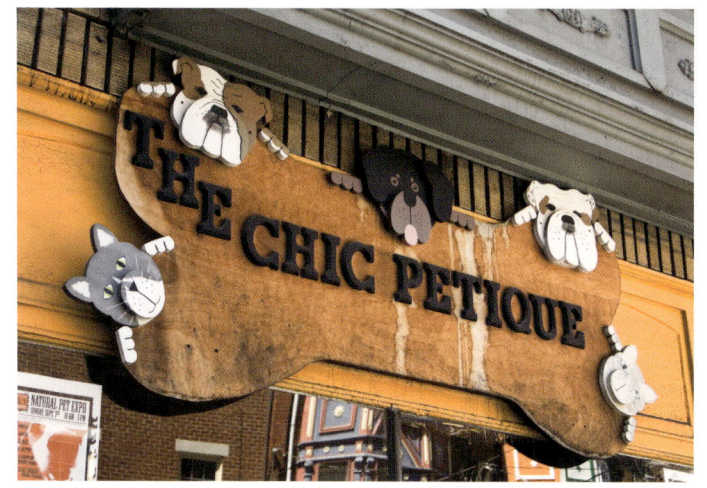

ピアス Warrior (Piercing , Philadelphia)

ペットショップ The Chic petique (Pet shop , Philadelphia)

グッズ Character (Goods , New York)

チャイルドケア The Red threads (Child care , New York)

食品店 Quick shop market (Grocery store , Miami)

葉巻店 Unknown (Cigar store , Miami)

博物館 Fireman's hall (Museum , Philadelphia)

Street furniture & Other

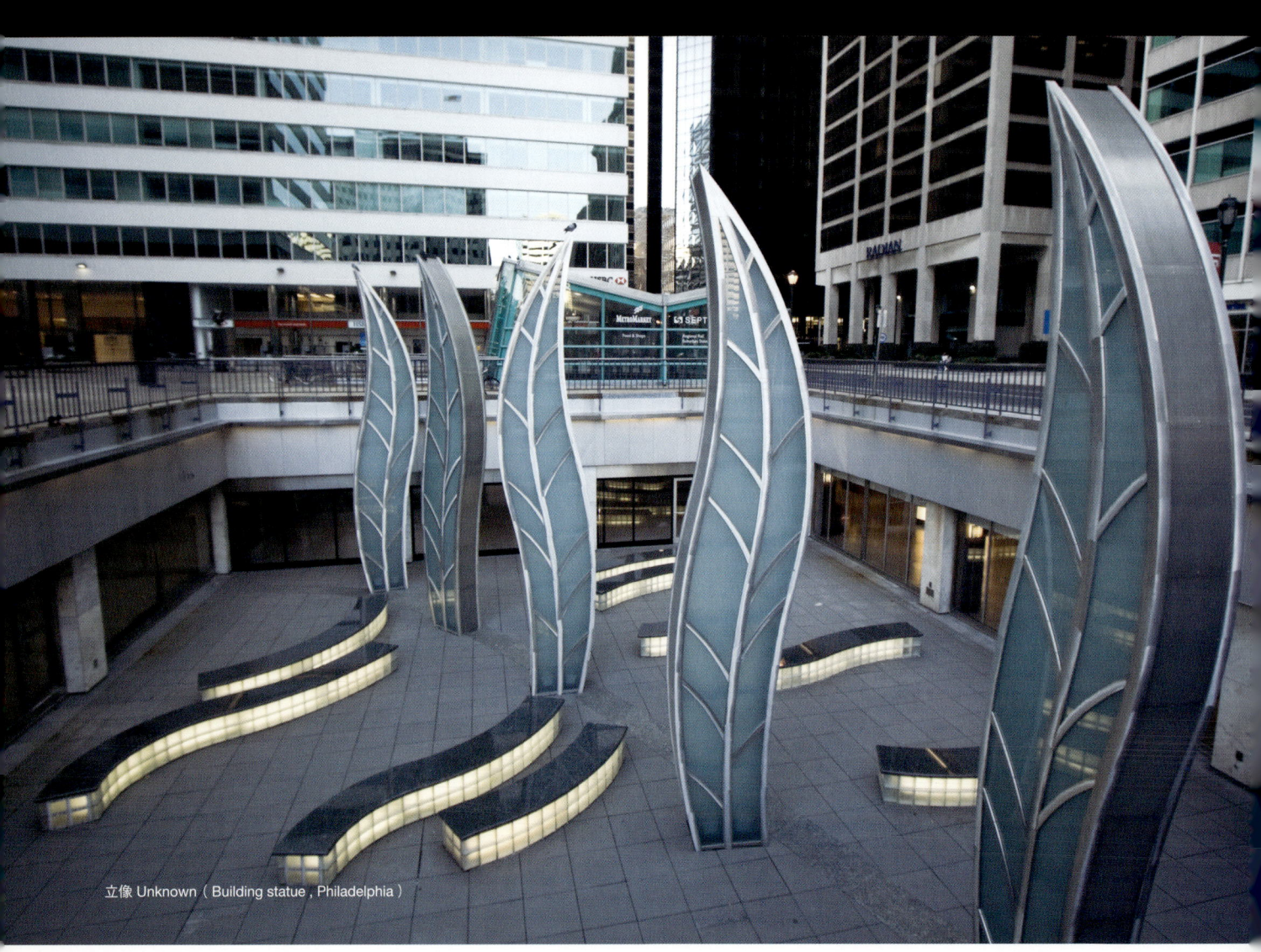

立像 Unknown (Building statue , Philadelphia)

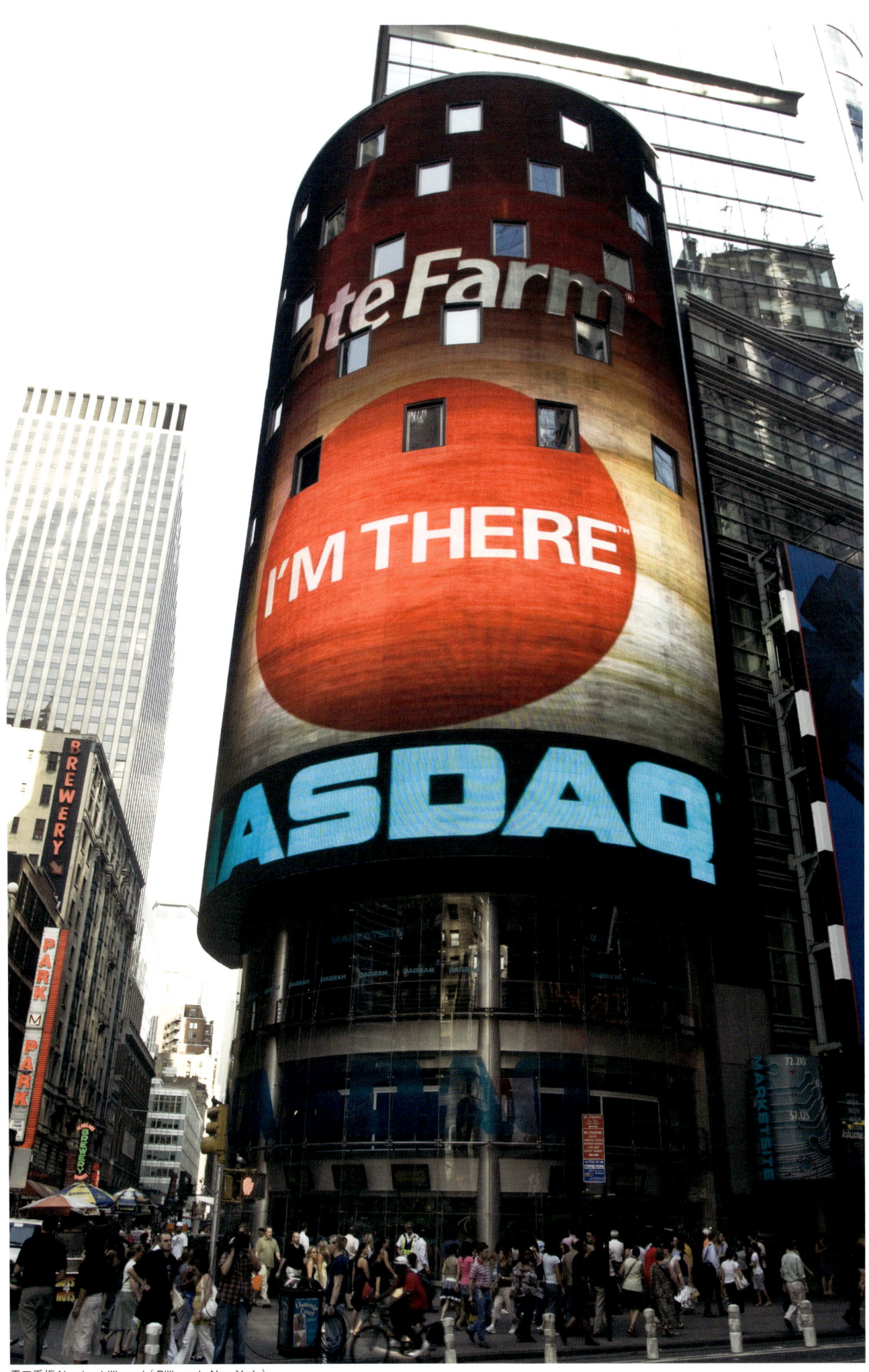

電工看板 Nasdaq billboard（Billboard, New York）

バス停 Bus stop（Miami）

バス停 Bus stop（New York）

バス停 Bus stop（Philadelphia）

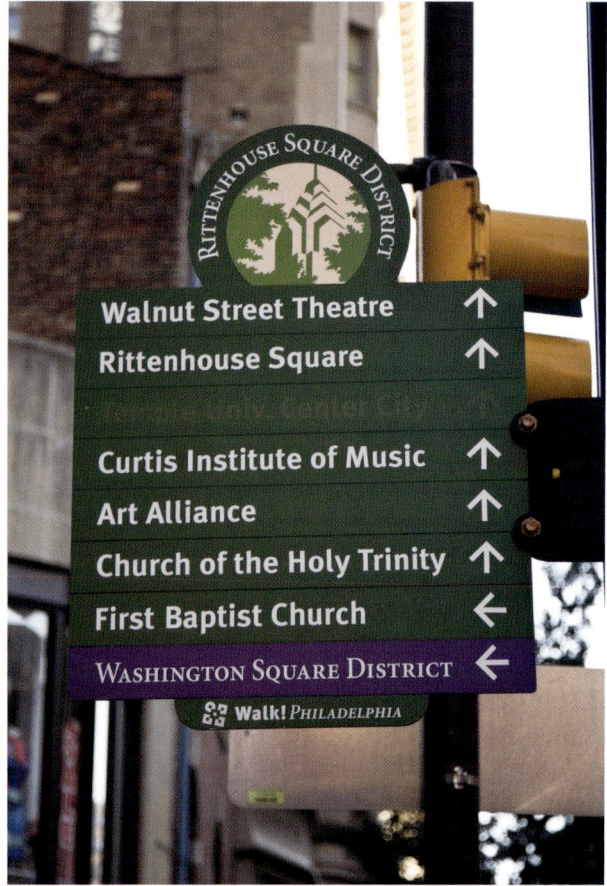

エリアディレクション Area direction（Philadelphia）

通り案内 Street sign（Miami）

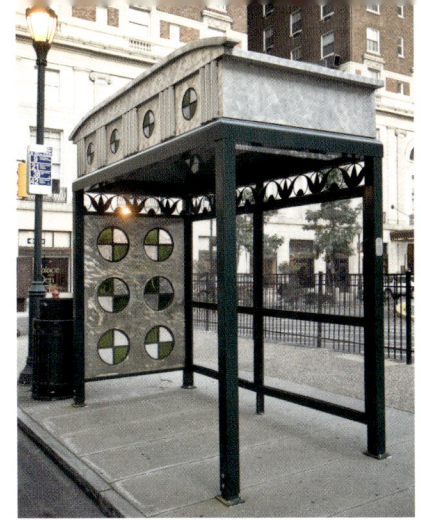

バス停 Bus stop（Philadelphia）

バス停 Bus stop（New York）

バスマップ Bus map（Philadelphia）

広告塔 Mary Brickell village（Area event AD , Miami）

エリアマップ Area map（Philadelphia）

エリアマップ Area map（Philadelphia）

パーキング Park（Philadelphia）

ビルディレクトリー Building directory（Philadelphia）

駐車料金支払機 Parking vender（Miami）

エリアマップ Area map（Philadelphia）

パーキングサイン Park sign（Philadelphia）

交通案内 Traffic sign（Miami）

エリアマップ Area map (New York)

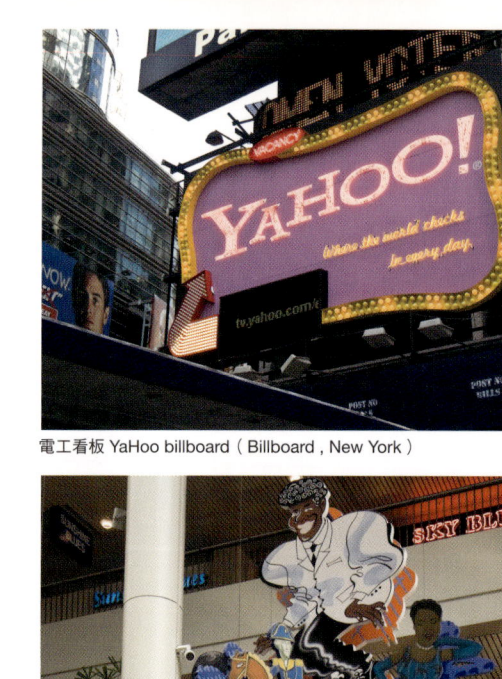

電工看板 YaHoo billboard (Billboard , New York)

モール案内 Broad street mall (Mall map , Philadelphia)

モール案内 Broad street mall (Mall map , Philadelphia)

看板 M&M Sign (New York)

ディレクトリー Directory（Miami）

広告塔 Top of the rock AD board（New York）

広告塔 AD Board（Miami）

エリアサイン Phlash（Area sign, Philadelphia）

マイアミ観光案内所 Miami visitors center（Miami）

チケット売り場 Ticket vender（New York）

交通標識 Traffic sign（Miami）

エリア案内 Mary Brickell village（Area sign, Miami）

公園電灯 Park light post（Miami）

新聞販売機 Newspaper vender（Miami）

新聞販売機 Newspaper vender（New York）

ゴミ箱 Trash can（Miami）

ゴミ箱 Trash can（Philadelphia）

水飲み場 Park faucet（New York）

ベンチ Bench chair（Miami）

ベンチ Bench chair（Miami）